My Adventu~To~ Curwood Castle

My Adventure To Curwood Castle

Special thanks to: *Cherie and Annora Teed for the character inspirations.*

First printing, 2019

Publisher, Edward O. Rigdon, i Flip Digital, 5188 N M52, Owosso, MI 48867

www.iflipdigital.com

One day, my mom asked me if I wanted to go to a museum. She told me we had some extra time today and that it would be a fun trip. She also said it was a very special place she visited when she was young.

A museum? I thought museums were full of old dusty things that people didn't want anymore. I can't imagine why we would go to a place like that.

My mom started laughing and said, "No, museums are full of history, art and culture. The museum we are going to is a very nice place to visit."
So off we went to visit the museum.

Wow, what a surprise! When we arrived, the museum was in a castle! There was a sign out front telling about James Oliver Curwood and his castle.

CURWOOD CASTLE

James Oliver Curwood was born in Owosso on June 12, 1878, and lived here most of his life. Writing and love of nature were his boyhood interests, and by 1908 Curwood was earning his living as a novelist. Most of his stories were adventure tales set in the Canadian north, where the author spent much of his time. During the 1920s his books were among the most popular in North America, and many were made into movies. The castle, built in 1922, was his writing studio, and a number of his later works were composed in the tower, overlooking the Shiawassee River. Curwood became a zealous conservationist, and in 1926 he was appointed to the Michigan Conservation Commission. He died at his nearby home on Williams Street on August 13, 1927.

I was so excited to see a castle, I started sprinting for the front door. On my way I saw a statue standing next to the river, so I decided to take a look.

It was a bronze statue of James Oliver Curwood! Mom said, "He was an American action-adventure writer. He built the castle as a studio back in 1922 to write his stories. He loved nature and the outdoors."

AUTHOR :JAMES OLIVER CURWOOD 1878-1927
ARTIST : RYAN RAY LESLIE 1986-2011

I found a boat landing that belongs to the castle. I'm sure it was used quite often back when Mr. Curwood had friends and family gathered here.

I was in such a big hurry to see what was inside the castle and in Curwood Castle Park, I almost missed the sign out front that said the castle was open today!

Next, I tried to count all the stones on the castle. It was too hard to count them all, so I decided to explore the inside of the castle instead.

Before I got to the door, I saw a big rock with a plaque on it. It was a memorial to James Oliver Curwood for his work as a conservationist. A conservationist is a person who works to protect animals and the earth.

THE STUDIO
OF
JAMES OLIVER CURWOOD
AUTHOR AND MICHIGAN'S
FOREMOST CONSERVATIONIST
BORN JUNE 12, 1878
DIED AUGUST 13, 1927

TABLET ERECTED 1938   OWOSSO CENTENNIAL

I was very excited to go inside and explore, but I had to wait for my mom to catch up with me. I really didn't want to go inside alone. I was afraid I might miss something important.

Mom was talking to the castle's caretaker. She wanted to ask her some questions, so I walked into the Great Room to explore a little. I found a big fireplace with a huge moose head hanging above it.

We went into the basement and saw some of Mr. Curwood's books and movie items. There were a lot of great things to see. The walls were decorated with movie posters that were based on some of his stories.

Before I went back up the basement stairs, I stopped and pondered over all the achievements Mr. Curwood accomplished in his life-time. He must have had a wonderful imagination to create all those amazing stories.

On the first floor of the turret was the room Mr. Curwood liked to write in. He was a very accomplished author that wrote many articles, magazines, books, stories, and films.

One of my favorite round rooms in the turret was the one with the porthole windows. It was just like being in a big ship. The room also had some items that belonged to Mr. Curwood.

I had a lot of fun going up and down all the spiral stairways in the turret. I was able to visit all of the round rooms. As I went through each of the rooms, I wondered which one might have been Mr. Curwood's favorite.

I'm sure the top of the turret was a place Mr. Curwood enjoyed. The room had a great view of Owosso and the Shiawassee River. There were many things from his past on display. I even saw photographs of his family and some of his everyday items he used when writing.

When I looked out of the turret windows, I was hoping to see some of the same things Mr. Curwood saw when he looked out of them. I saw the river really well from up there. I could understand why he liked the turret so much.

My mom told me how important James Oliver Curwood is to Owosso's history. She wanted me to know that places like Curwood Castle need to be taken care of so other people can visit and enjoy them too.

This was a great adventure! I found out James Oliver Curwood was a famous author that loved nature. He had the castle built on the banks of the Shiawassee River so he could use it as a studio to write his stories. I hope you search for more historical treasures in the area!

Fun Activity Questions for
Your Adventure To Curwood Castle!

1. Were you able to find a weather vain on one of the turrets?

2. What did the statue of James Oliver Curwood have in its hands?

3. How many stones do you estimate were on the exterior of the castle?

4. Which room had the most books on display?

5. How many posters did you count in the castle? Which was your favorite?

6. How many typewriters did you see?

7. Can you name three other items you saw that Mr. Curwood used for writing?

8. What room do you think had the best view of the Shiawassee River?

9. How many levels did you count in the castle?

10. How many steps did you count in the castle?

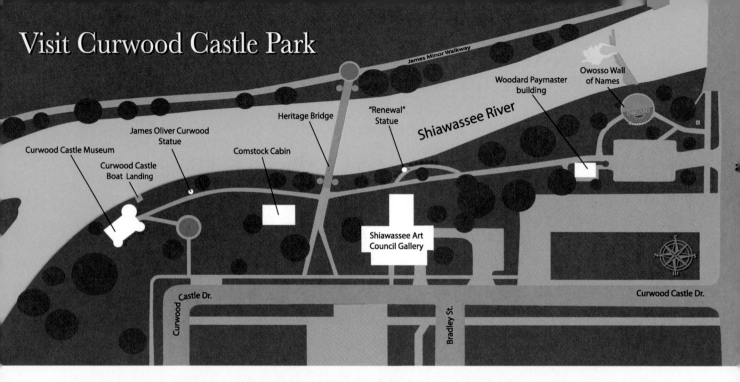

Visit Curwood Castle Park

James Minor Walkway

Woodard Paymaster building

Owosso Wall of Names

"Renewal" Statue

Shiawassee River

Heritage Bridge

James Oliver Curwood Statue

Curwood Castle Museum

Comstock Cabin

Curwood Castle Boat Landing

Shiawassee Art Council Gallery

Curwood Castle Dr.

Bradley St.

Curwood Castle Dr.

Making Your Visit to Curwood Castle Park Special!

Always be prepared if you are making a journey! If your planning on taking your own adventure to Curwood Castle Park, remember to call ahead or visit the website for general information. It includes the hours for the Curwood Castle Museum and the Shiawassee Art Council building. The site also includes the Curwood Festival dates and any other special events in the area.

For More Information Contact:
Owosso Historical Commission, Call: 989-723-2155 Website: Owossohistory.org
Shiawassee Art Center, Call: 989-723-8354 Website: Shiawasseearts.org

37438899R00015

Made in the USA
Middletown, DE
27 February 2019